I0606135
THE NORDIC REGION
FINLAND
KATIE GILLESPIE
AV2
www.openlightbox.com

Step 1
Go to **www.openlightbox.com**

Step 2
Enter this unique code
OQMLTB3Y1

Step 3
Explore your interactive eBook!

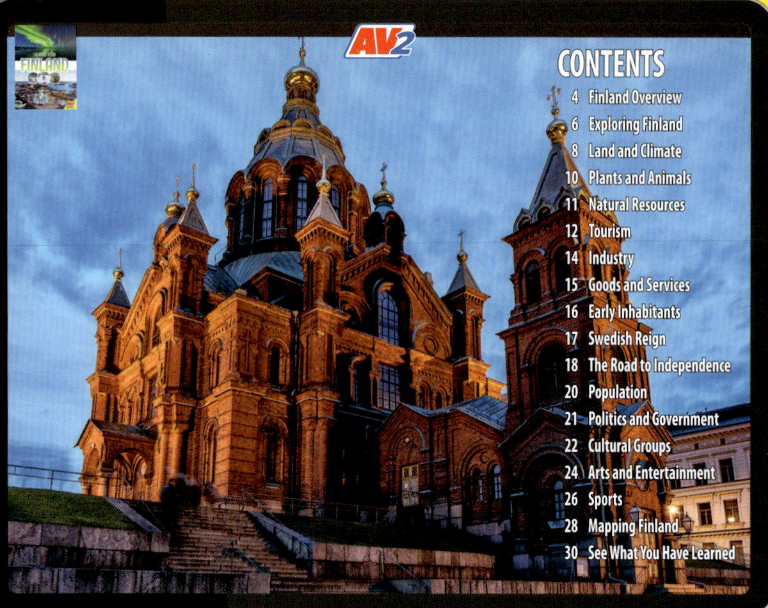

AV2 is optimized for use on any device

Your interactive eBook comes with...

Contents
Browse a live contents page to easily navigate through resources

Audio
Listen to sections of the book read aloud

Videos
Watch informative video clips

Weblinks
Gain additional information for research

Slideshows
View images and captions

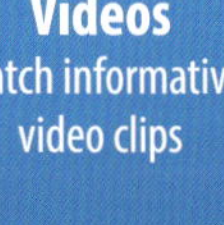

Try This!
Complete activities and hands-on experiments

Key Words
Study vocabulary, and complete a matching word activity

Quizzes
Test your knowledge

Share
Share titles within your Learning Management System (LMS) or Library Circulation System

Citation
Create bibliographical references following APA, CMOS, and MLA styles

This title is part of our AV2 digital subscription

1-Year 3–8 Subscription
ISBN 978-1-7911-3306-1

Access hundreds of AV2 titles with our digital subscription.
Sign up for a FREE trial at **www.openlightbox.com/trial**

The digital components of this book are guaranteed to stay active for at least five years from the date of publication.

THE NORDIC REGION

FINLAND

Contents

Finland Overview

Finland is a country in northern Europe. Along with Iceland, Sweden, Denmark, and Norway, it is part of the Nordic region. Finland is the northernmost country in the **European Union (EU)**. The people who live there are known as Finns. Finland provides its people with a high standard of living. In terms of employment, education, safety, and environmental quality, the country ranks among the best in the world. In 2022, the World Happiness Report named Finland the happiest country on Earth for the fifth consecutive year.

Focus on Finland

Capital
Helsinki

Population
5.6 million

Currency
Euro

National Coat of Arms

National Flag

National Anthem
"Maamme" ("Our Land")

National Animal
Brown Bear

National Flower
Lily-of-the-Valley

National Bird
Whooper Swan

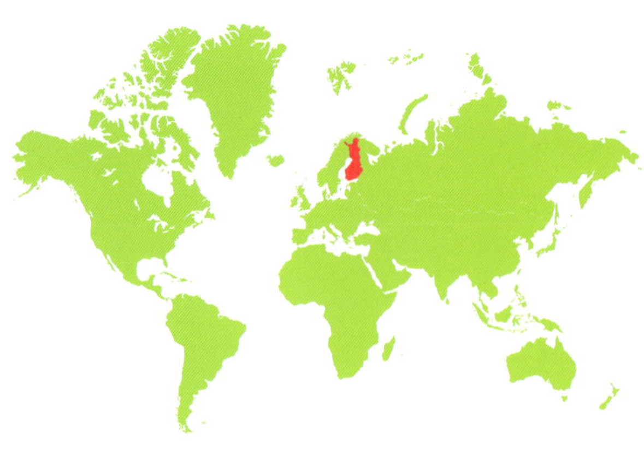

Finland covers an area of about 131,000 square miles (339,000 square kilometers). Located between Sweden and Russia, it acts as a symbolic border dividing northeastern and northwestern Europe. About one-third of the country lies north of the **Arctic Circle**. Finland shares land borders with two other Nordic countries. These are Norway in the north and Sweden in the northwest. Russia borders Finland to the east. The Gulf of Bothnia, Baltic Sea, and Gulf of Finland make up Finland's coastal borders.

Nordic Region Map

ARCTIC OCEAN
Mount Halti
WHITE SEA
NORWEGIAN SEA
FINLAND
SWEDEN
Salpausselkä Ridges
Lake Saimaa
RUSSIA
Gulf of Bothnia
Helsinki
Gulf of Finland
NORWAY
ESTONIA
BALTIC SEA
LATVIA

Map Legend
Finland
Salpausselkä Ridges
Mount Halti
Lake Saimaa
Helsinki
Land
Water
N W E S
SCALE 100 mi 100 km

Helsinki

Helsinki is Finland's largest city. It was founded in 1550. However, it did not become the country's capital until 1812. Helsinki is the northernmost capital in continental Europe.

Lake Saimaa

Lake Saimaa is the largest lake in Finland. It is also the fourth-largest lake in Europe. Saimaa covers 1,700 square miles (4,400 square km). It is a popular tourist destination.

Mount Halti

With an **elevation** of 4,357 feet (1,328 meters), Mount Halti is Finland's highest mountain. It is found in the Haltia, Finland's only mountain range. The range runs along the Finland-Norway border.

Salpausselkä Ridges

Southern Finland's Salpausselkä ridges are one of the country's most unique geological features. These three **parallel** ridges formed thousands of years ago. They are about 310 miles (500 km) long.

Land and Climate

Finland is the seventh-largest country in Europe. It is almost the same size as the U.S. state of Montana. From north to south, Finland extends 721 miles (1,160 km) in length. Its maximum width is 336 miles (540 km) from east to west.

The country can be divided into four distinct geographic regions. Archipelago Finland includes the thousands of islands that surround the southern mainland. Coastal Finland extends inland from the coast and is made up mostly of flat plains. This is Finland's main agricultural area. The Lake District is the country's largest geographic region. Located in the interior of the country, it is home to most of the country's 188,000 lakes. The Upland Forest region makes up the northern part of the country and includes land north of the Arctic Circle.

Forests cover about 70 percent of Finland. Many are contained within national parks such as northern Finland's Oulanka National Park.

Finland has a continental climate. This means that it has significant temperature changes between seasons. Finland is colder than other countries in the Nordic region. However, it is still generally milder than most other places that lie as far north, such as Alaska. Much of this is due to air flow from the Atlantic Ocean, which is itself warmed by the **Gulf Stream**.

Winters in Finland are long and cold, especially north of the Arctic Circle. Here, temperatures can drop to –22° Fahrenheit (–30° Celsius). Snow is common. There is little or no sunshine. Farther south, winters are milder. However, temperatures still hover around freezing.

Finland's summers are short, but come with days that are long and sunny. The weather is typically mild and rainy. Depending on the area, temperatures can reach as high as 80°F (27°C).

In northern Finland, the annual precipitation is about 16 to 26 inches (40 to 65 centimeters). Figures are slightly higher in the southern part of the country. Here, precipitation ranges from 28 to 30 inches (70 to 75 cm). Spring is Finland's driest season. Summer and autumn are its wettest.

Seasonal Finland

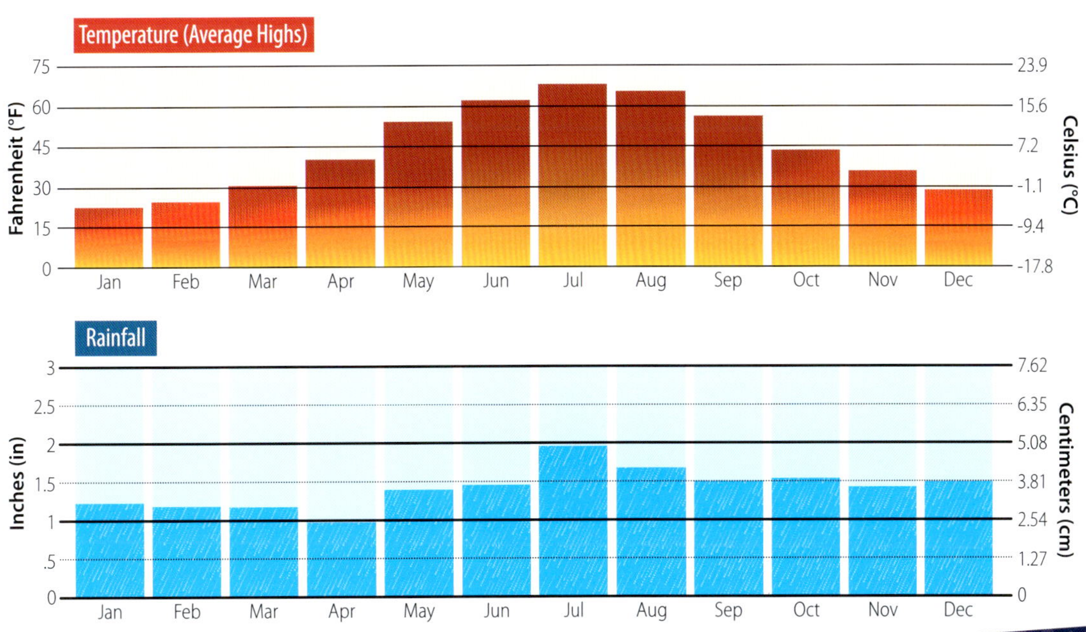

Plants and Animals

Known for the purplish tint it has when young, the blewit is one of hundreds of wild mushroom species that grow in Finland.

Most of Finland's forests are filled with **coniferous** trees. These are mainly pine and spruce. **Deciduous** birch trees are also common. **Lichens** often grow in the northern part of the country. There are also more than 1,000 **species** of flowering plants.

Finland is home to a wide variety of animals, too. Reindeer live in the northern region of Lapland. Ducks and other waterfowl reside in the country's lakes. Lynxes, moose, and wolves dwell in the woods. Fur animals such as beavers, ermines, and minks are plentiful. Marine life includes harbor porpoises and white whales. Pike, perch, and salmon are among the fish found in Finland's waters. Seabirds such as the black-backed gull and Arctic tern can be found along the coastal islands.

One of Finland's most interesting animals is the Saimaa ringed seal. These seals can remain underwater for more than 20 minutes at a time. They eat about 2,200 pounds (1,000 kilograms) of fish per year. Each seal's fur pattern is different and is as distinctive as a human fingerprint. Found exclusively in the Saimaa lake system, this seal is endangered. Its population is only about 410.

Finland is home to more than 900 breeding-age golden eagles. Most are found in the northern part of the country.

A full-grown Saimaa seal can reach a length of about 5 feet (152 centimeters) and weigh about 200 pounds (90 kilograms).

Natural Resources

Approximately 80 percent of Finland's timber comes from privately owned forests.

With its abundance of forests, it is no surprise that trees are Finland's top natural resource. Various forest products are made from these trees. They include sawn timber, pulp, and paper.

Forests also provide energy for the country. About 30 percent of Finland's total energy consumption comes from its forests. Most of this energy is produced using waste products such as sawdust and bark.

Finland uses other natural resources to produce energy as well. Much of its power comes from its rivers, in the form of **hydroelectricity**. In fact, the country has more than 300 hydroelectric plants. Other natural sources of power generation include wind, **geothermal** energy, and peat.

The country is also rich in mineral resources. Among these are iron ore, zinc, copper, cobalt, chromium, and nickel. Most of Finland's mines are located in the northern part of the country.

The Imatra hydropower plant is Finland's largest. Located in the eastern part of the country, its annual output provides electricity for more than 50,000 homes.

Tourism

Finland welcomes visitors from around the globe. Almost 900,000 tourists visited the country in 2020. They spent more than $1.75 billion.

The country offers its guests a variety of unique experiences. Some come to try a traditional Finnish **sauna**. Others want to experience the region's natural beauty by visiting one of the country's 41 national parks. The **northern lights** are another draw. People will often head to the great outdoors on a clear night to watch the lights dancing in the sky.

Thrill seekers will enjoy Tampere's Särkänniemi Theme Park. Its more than 30 rides include a roller coaster, drop tower, and **rapids** ride. Santa Claus Village, in Rovaniemi is another popular amusement park. Situated on the Arctic Circle, it is advertised as the home of Father Christmas.

Finland has a number of museums. With exhibits ranging from history to science, there is something for everyone. Turku Castle was originally a military fortress. Today, it is a museum devoted to the history of the Nordic region. Visitors to Inari can learn about Sámi culture at the Sámi Museum Siida and Sámi Cultural Centre. The Sámi are the only **Indigenous people** within the EU. Science lovers will enjoy the Rovaniemi's Arktikum Science Centre. Art lovers can wander through the rooms of the Finnish National Gallery, in Helsinki. It is the country's largest art museum organization.

The Sibelius sculpture in Helsinki was created by Finnish sculptor Eila Hiltunen. Unveiled in 1967, its highest pipe reaches more than 27 feet (8 m) into the air.

The Santa Office is one of the most important buildings at Santa Claus Village. It is here that visitors can meet Santa Claus and watch his elves build toys and other gifts for Christmas.

Known for its dedication to musical pursuits, Finland hosts countless festivals throughout the year. Olavinlinna Castle is known for its opera festival. Tampere is renowned for its Tampere Jazz Happening. Vaasa, reported to be the sunniest town in Finland, is home to the Korsholm Music Festival and Vaasa Choir Festival.

Jean Sibelius is probably Finland's best-known composer. Over the course of his career, he composed works ranging from concertos to symphonies. Visitors to his hometown of Hämeenlinna can learn more about the composer, as well as the history of Finnish music, at the Sibelius Museum. Helsinki's Sibelius Park features a monument built in honor of the composer. An impressive sight, the Sibelius Monument features 600 steel organ pipes.

Industry

Finland has a **gross domestic product (GDP)** of almost $300 billion. This comes mainly from **service industries**, manufacturing, and refining. Although they have declined in recent years, agriculture and fishing contribute to Finland's economy as well.

Known today for its electronics equipment, Nokia was founded in 1865 to produce paper products in southern Finland.

Manufacturing is one of the top industries in Finland. It employs more than 350,000 people. The country is renowned for producing electronics, machinery, ships, chemicals, and forest products.

About 6,600 people are employed by Finland's fishing industry, which includes fishing, **aquaculture**, and processing. The majority of these people are either inland or marine fishers. The country's **fish landings** total approximately 107,000 tons (97,000 metric tons). Included in this catch are whitefish, pike, char, sea and rainbow trout, and salmon.

Planting crops is only possible in certain parts of the country. This is due to Finland's cold climate and short growing season. However, many farmers raise animals. Pigs and reindeer are popular choices, as are animals that produce furs, such as minks and foxes.

Finland GDP by Sector

The majority of Finland's GDP comes from the service sector. Industry makes up about one-quarter. Agriculture accounts for only a small portion of the GDP.

71.6%
Services

25.6%
Industry

2.8%
Agriculture

Goods and Services

Finland has approximately 250 hospitals to serve the healthcare needs of its citizens. Some of these hospitals are specialized, such as Helsinki's Children's Hospital, which opened its doors in 2018.

Nearly 75 percent of Finns are employed in the service sector. These jobs are in a variety of fields. Some of the largest are healthcare, social work, and education.

The country's economy is dependent on trade with other nations. In 2021, Finland **exported** more than $81 billion worth of products. Major export items are computers, paper, wood, electrical equipment, iron, and steel.

Finland also **imports** many goods. These include machinery, smartphones, and cars. Its largest category of imports is fossil fuels, as there are no natural sources of oil in the country. Imported mineral fuels include both crude and processed oil, in addition to electrical energy, coal, and petroleum gas.

Finland has been a member of the EU since 1995. As part of the EU, it relies on trade with other EU countries. These include its Nordic neighbors, Sweden and Denmark, as well as Germany and the Netherlands. Finland has also developed trade relationships with the other countries in the Nordic region. Outside of Europe, Finland's top trading partners are China and the United States.

One of Finland's largest container ports is located in Helsinki. In 2021 alone, more than 15 million tons (14 million metric tons) of cargo passed through the port.

Early Inhabitants

The first people to live in what is now Finland arrived during the **Stone Age**. They came to the area in about 9000 BC. These people were most likely led to the region while following fish and game. Several different tribes moved into the area, and it is believed that at least one group were the ancestors of the Sámi.

Between 75,000 and 100,000 Sámi currently live in the Nordic region. Finland is home to about 10,000 of these people.

About 3,000 years later, another tribe arrived from the southeast. These people spoke a Finno-Ugric language. Today, this language family includes modern-day Finnish, as well as related languages such as Estonian and Hungarian. Other groups followed soon after. They adopted this language as well.

By 1000 BC, more people had moved to the area, including the ancestors of the present-day Finns. Agriculture and fishing were common ways of life. As different groups met and interacted, their settlements spread across the country. Over time, the Sámi were forced northward. Other tribes moved south.

Archaeologists have found a variety of artifacts relating to prehistoric Finland, including pottery. These artifacts have helped them gain deeper understanding of Finland's early peoples.

Swedish Reign

Until the mid-12th century, Finland was not ruled by any single entity. In 1157, it was conquered by King Erik IX during the first Swedish **crusade**. Finland became part of the Swedish kingdom. Christianity was introduced to the people, as was the Swedish language. Swedish became the dominant language of the land.

Other countries were also interested in Finland. Denmark and Russia both fought with Sweden for control of the area. After years of invasions and counterattacks, an agreement was finally reached. Approved in 1323, it ended the crusades. It also defined Finland as part of Sweden.

Over the next few centuries, Finland remained under Swedish rule. Cities were established. The Finns fought in many wars on behalf of Sweden. However, in the 18th century, Sweden lost its position of power. During the Great Northern War (1700–1721), Russia was able to move into southeastern Finland and set up an **occupation**. The treaty that ended the war saw Sweden **cede** that part of Finland to Russia.

King Erik IX ruled Sweden from 1155 until 1160. His efforts to expand his realm and the Christian religion earned him a sainthood in the years following his death.

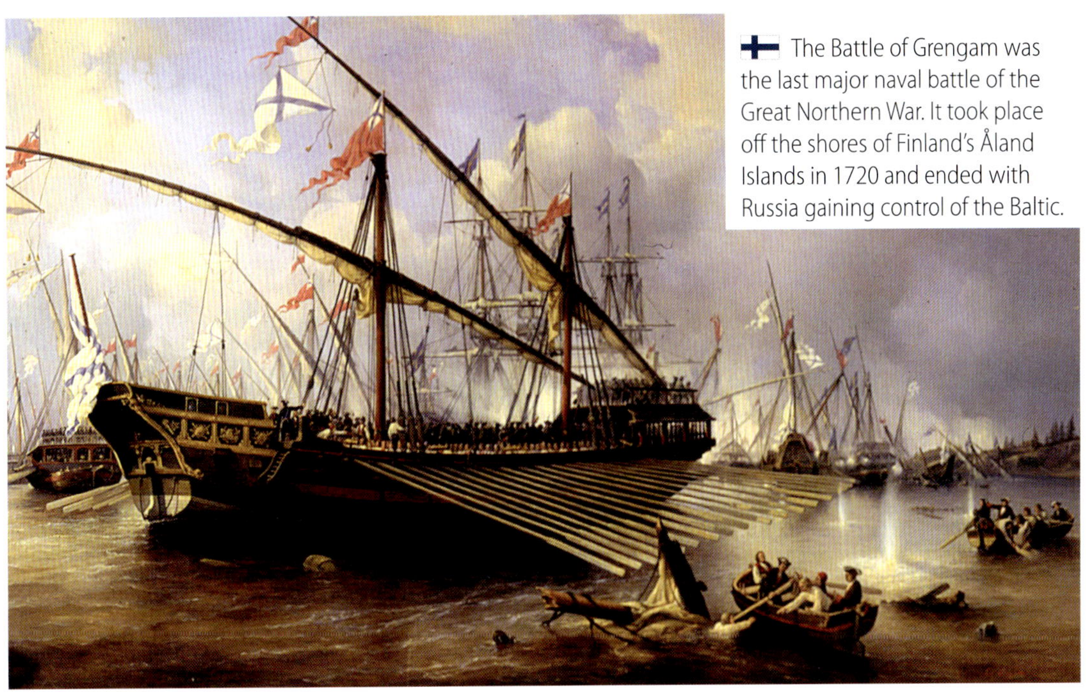

The Battle of Grengam was the last major naval battle of the Great Northern War. It took place off the shores of Finland's Åland Islands in 1720 and ended with Russia gaining control of the Baltic.

The Road to Independence

The Russian presence in southern Finland put the rest of the country in a vulnerable position. The threat of another invasion was always present, as Russia continued to exert pressure on Sweden's claim to the land. In 1808, the situation finally erupted into what is now known as the War of Finland. Within a year, Russia had won the war and taken control of Finland.

Rather than **annexing** Finland as a province of the Russian Empire, Russia's emperor, Tsar Alexander I, made the Finns an offer. He proposed that Finland become a grand duchy of Russia. This would make it an **autonomous** state. Finland's laws would not change. It would not have to pay taxes. Its religion would be respected. Individual rights would remain intact, as would Finland's inherited traditions.

Finland agreed to this proposal and became a grand duchy in 1809. The emperor selected a group of officials to govern Finland on his behalf. The country was run by this **bureaucracy** until 1863. During this time, several reforms were carried out. These included returning southeastern Finland back to the country and making Finnish one of the duchy's official languages.

More changes took place after Tsar Alexander II became Russia's ruler. In 1863, he dissolved the bureaucracy and allowed Finland to form its own government. The tsar also brought forward a new act to ensure that the assembly meet on a regular basis. This led to the Conscription Act of 1878, which gave Finland its own army.

All of these steps fueled a sense of **nationalism** in the Finnish people. On December 6, 1917, Finland's Parliament declared the country's independence from Russia. This was recognized by the Russian government later that year.

Although the separation from Russia was peaceful, **civil war** broke out in Finland shortly after its declaration of independence. The war was bloody, but ended in May 1918. The following year, Finland became a **republic**. Kaarlo Juho Ståhlberg was elected the country's first president.

In 1812, Alexander I named Helsinki the capital of Finland. At the time, the city had a population of about 4,000. By the end of the century, that number had grown to more than 60,000.

Finland's historic connections to Russia can be found throughout the country. Completed in 1868, the Uspenski Cathedral, in Helsinki, is the largest Eastern Orthodox church in Western Europe. Eastern Orthodox has long been the dominant religion of Russia.

Population

More than 5.5 million people live in Finland. However, it is one of the least densely populated countries in the EU. Finland only has about 43 people per square mile (16 people per square km). This is much less than the United States, which has a population density of about 94 people per square mile (36 people per square km).

Finland's population is slowly increasing. By 2030, the country is expected to have more than 5.7 million residents.

The majority of Finnish people, more than 85 percent, reside in **urban** areas. While the population of Helsinki is approximately 650,000, its metropolitan area is home to about 1.3 million people. Finland's second-largest city is Espoo. It has nearly 300,000 people. Tampere ranks third, with a population of more than 240,000.

Since 1990, **immigration** to Finland has increased. Most immigrants have come from Russia, Sweden, Estonia, and Somalia. Over the past decade, Finland has welcomed between 26,000 and 36,000 immigrants per year. In 2021, the country set a record. It had a total of 36,364 registered immigrants.

Finland Age Groups

About two-thirds of Finland's population is between 15 and 64 years old. The remaining third is split almost evenly above and below this range, with slightly more people 65 or older.

15.5%

Age 0–14 years

61.6%

Age 15–64 years

22.9%

Age 65+ years

Politics and Government

Finland has remained a republic to this day. It is led by a president, who acts as the **head of state**. Sauli Niinistö has been Finland's president since 2012. The country has a prime minister as well, who serves as the head of government. Sanna Marin became prime minister of Finland in 2019. She is the youngest person ever to hold this position.

Finland is also a **parliamentary democracy**. The parliament, or Eduskunta, has a single legislative chamber of 200 elected members. Their terms last for four years.

The fundamental rules, principles, and values of Finnish society are detailed in the country's constitution. It also outlines the powers of the country's three branches of government. The executive branch exercises governmental powers. These powers are divided between the president and the prime minister. The Eduskunta is the legislative branch. Among its responsibilities are approving the nation's budget, electing the prime minister, and overseeing the government. The judicial branch passes judgments in disputes. It includes district courts, courts of appeal, and the supreme court.

Sanna Marin was first elected to the Finnish parliament in 2015 as a member of the country's Social Democratic Party. She became leader of that party in 2020.

Finland's Parliament House was inaugurated in 1931. Since then, it has been the center of the country's political life.

Cultural Groups

The majority of Finland's people are **ethnic** Finns. Although they share a common culture, Finns are sometimes divided into Eastern and Western groups. Eastern Finns are influenced by Karelia, a region in Russia. Western Finns are influenced by Sweden, as well as the other Scandinavian countries of Denmark and Norway.

There are few minority groups in Finland. In fact, only about 8.5 percent of the country's population have a foreign background. They include people from Sweden, Russia, and Estonia.

Although there are many languages spoken in Finland, only two are official. These are Finnish and Swedish. More than 85 percent of the population speaks Finnish. About 5 percent speak Swedish. These people live primarily in the Åland Islands and coastal areas of southern and western Finland. Russian-speakers make up about 1.5 percent of the country's population. Among the other languages spoken in Finland are Estonian, English, Roma, and Sámi.

Like most Scandinavian countries, Finland's history is intertwined with the Vikings, warriors who staged raids and built settlements throughout much of Europe. Every July, the Åland Islands celebrate their links to Viking culture with the Viking Market. Guests can watch recreations of Viking battles, purchase Viking-themed crafts, and eat Viking-style food.

Christianity was established as Finland's main religion by the 13th century. For many years, the country was mainly Roman Catholic. In 1593, another branch of Christianity, called Lutheranism, became Finland's official religion. Today, more than two-thirds of Finns are Lutheran. Most belong to the country's national church, *Suomen Evankelis-luterilainen kirkko*, or the Evangelical Lutheran Church of Finland.

A small number of Finns, roughly 1.1 percent, are Orthodox. This is the only other faith in the country with a national church. Other religious groups include the Pentecostals, Roman Catholics, and Buddhists. Finland has small Islamic and Jewish communities as well.

Turku Cathedral is the mother church of the Evangelical Lutheran Church of Finland. It has been serving its congregation since June 17, 1300.

Arts and Entertainment

Many entertainers hail from Finland. The country has produced a number of renowned writers, musicians, actors, actresses, directors, and other creators. They have impressed audiences for decades.

Author Aleksis Kivi is acknowledged as the father of the Finnish novel. His work *Seitsemän veljestä*, or *Seven Brothers*, was the first novel written in Finnish. It took Kivi 10 years to write this novel. It was published in 1870. Today, the anniversary of his birth is celebrated as Finnish Literature Day.

Another famous Finn, Tove Jansson, is beloved for her creation of the Moomin books. She both wrote and illustrated this acclaimed children's series. The books have been translated into more than 50 languages, making Jansson one of the most widely read Finnish authors abroad.

Tarja Turunen is one of Finland's top singers. This talented soprano from Kitee co-founded the symphonic metal band Nightwish. She also sang lead vocals. Helsinki native Michael Monroe is a singer and multi-instrumentalist. He is known for his work with Hanoi Rocks. The popular glam punk band has influenced musicians around the world.

Since leaving Nightwish in 2005, Tarja Turunen has been performing as a solo act, using only Tarja as her stage name.

Several Finns have found success in television and film. Actor Ville Virtanen starred in the crime drama *Bordertown*. Joonas Suotamo rose to fame for his role as Chewbacca in the *Star Wars* sequel trilogy. Director Renny Harlin is one of the best-known Finnish filmmakers in Hollywood. Among his most popular films are *Die Hard 2*, *Cutthroat Island*, and *Deep Blue Sea*.

The popularity of the Moomin books has led to the creation of a series of gift shops devoted to Moomin products, ranging from clothing to coffee mugs. Besides Finland, these stores can be found in countries such as England and the United States.

Helsinki's Linus Torvalds is one of the world's most famous software engineers. He created the Linux kernel in 1991. This was a fundamental achievement in the world of software development. Today, it is used in operating systems such as Android. His work has earned Torvalds numerous awards and a place in the Internet Hall of Fame.

Sports

Finland's national sport is called pesäpallo. Similar to baseball, the sport officially started a century ago, in 1922. Today, it is the country's second-most popular summer sport, after soccer, with more than 18,000 registered players.

In addition to pesäpallo, Finns enjoy a variety of other physical activities. Some of the most popular are skiing, ice hockey, motorsport, riding, fishing, and waterskiing. Soccer, or football, as it is known in Finland, is also well loved.

Cross-country skiing is not only a mode of transportation in Finland, it is also a competitive sport. Jesse Väänänen and Matias Strandvall are two of Finland's best cross-country skiers. Marja-Liisa Hämäläinen is a highly decorated legend of the sport. Among her many honors are seven Olympic and eight World Championship medals.

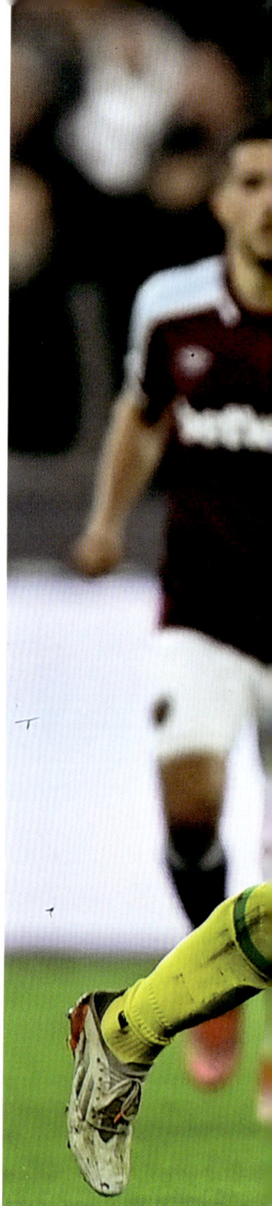

Espoo's Kimi Räikkönen is one of Finland's top racing drivers. He is nicknamed "The Iceman," for his calm demeanor on and off the track. Räikkönen began competing in Formula One (F1) in 2001. While driving for the McLaren team, he placed second in both the 2003 and 2005 Formula One Drivers' World Championships. In 2007, with team Ferrari, he took first place. After retiring from F1 in 2021, Räikkönen made a comeback racing for NASCAR in 2022.

Many soccer players come from Finland. One of the country's biggest stars is Teemu Pukki from Kotka. He currently plays for the Finland national team, as well as for Norwich City in the Premier League. This talented striker is the all-time leading Finnish goal scorer. He was named player of the season in the 2018–19 English Football League Championship.

Finland has a long Olympic history as well. It first competed at the Olympic Games in 1908, and hosted the summer games in 1952. Finnish athletes have earned almost 500 medals. The country's distance runners are especially well known. Lasse Virén, from Myrskylä, was the first person ever to win gold in both the 5,000-meter and 10,000-meter races at consecutive Olympics. Perhaps the most renowned Finnish runner is Helsinki's Paavo Nurmi. During the 1920s, he won a total of 12 Olympic medals. Three were silver and nine were gold.

Teemu Pukki has been a member of the Norwich City team since 2018. That same year, he was named the Player of the Season by the team's fans.

Over the course of his F1 career, Kimi Räikkönen won more than 20 Grand Prix races. He is considered to be the most successful driver to ever come out of Finland.

Mapping Finland

We use many tools to interpret maps and to understand the locations of features such as cities, states, lakes, and rivers. The map below has many tools to help interpret information on the map of Finland.

Finland Map

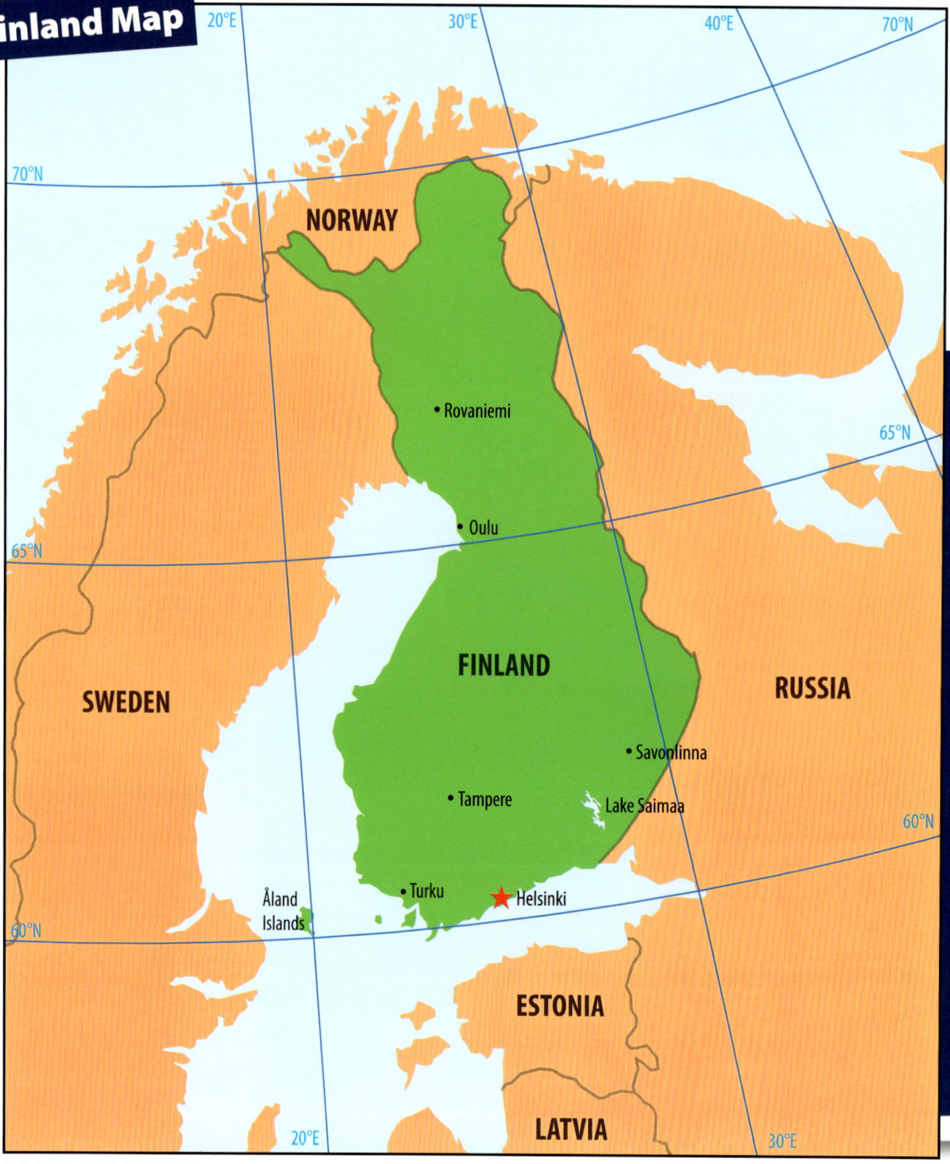

20°E
30°E
40°E
70°N
70°N
NORWAY
Rovaniemi
65°N
Oulu
65°N
FINLAND
RUSSIA
SWEDEN
Savonlinna
Tampere
Lake Saimaa
60°N
Turku
Helsinki
Åland Islands
60°N
ESTONIA
LATVIA
20°E
30°E

MAP LEGEND

Capital City
City
Body of Water
Country Border
Longitude & Latitude
Finland
Other Countries
N
W
E
S
SCALE
100 mi
100 km

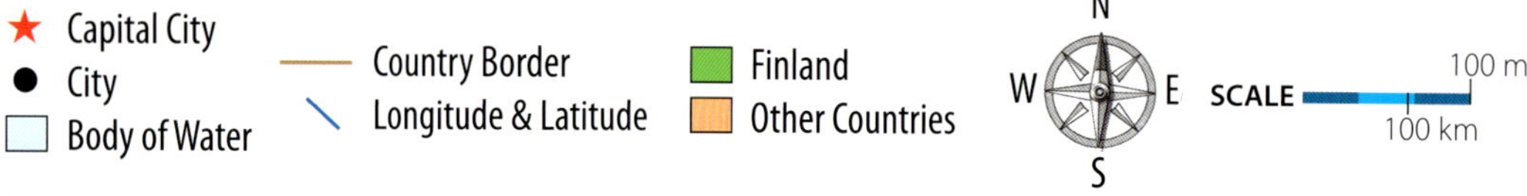

Mapping Tools

- The compass rose shows north, south, east, and west. The points in-between represent northeast, northwest, southeast, and southwest.
- The map scale shows that the distances on a map represent much longer distances in real life. If you measure the distance between objects on a map, you can use the map scale to calculate the actual distance in miles or kilometers between those two points.
- The lines of latitude and longitude are long lines that appear on maps. The lines of latitude run east to west and measure how far north or south of the equator a place is located. The lines of longitude run north to south and measure how far east or west of the Prime Meridian a place is located. A location on a map can be found by using the two numbers where latitude and longitude meet. This number is called a coordinate and is written using degrees and direction. For example, the city of Helsinki would be found at 60°N and 24°E on a map.

Map It!

Using the map and the appropriate tools, complete the activities below.

Locating with latitude and longitude

1. Which city is located at 60°N and 22°E?
2. Which body of water is located at 61°N and 28°E?
3. Which islands are located at 60°N and 20°E?

Distances between points

4. Using the map scale and a ruler, calculate the approximate distance between Oulu and Turku.
5. Using the map scale and a ruler, calculate the approximate distance between Helsinki and Tampere.
6. Using the map scale and a ruler, calculate the approximate distance between Rovaniemi and Savonlinna.

ANSWERS 1. Turku 2. Lake Saimaa 3. Åland Islands 4. 332 miles (534 km) 5. 111 miles (179 km) 6. 334 miles (537 km)

See What You Have Learned

Test your knowledge of Finland by answering these questions.

1 What is Finland's top natural resource?

2 What are Finland's two official languages?

3 What is the national flower of Finland?

4 In what year did Finland become a grand duchy of Russia?

5 In which city is the Finnish National Gallery?

6 How many Finns are employed in the manufacturing industry?

7 Which countries does Finland border?

8 What is Finland's national sport?

9 When did Finland become a member of the EU?

10 What is Finland's parliament called?

ANSWERS

1. Trees
2. Finnish and Swedish
3. Lily-of-the-Valley
4. 1809
5. Helsinki
6. More than 350,000
7. Norway, Sweden, and Russia
8. Pesäpallo
9. 1995
10. The Eduskunta

Key Words

annexing: taking possession of an area of land, typically by force and without permission
aquaculture: the farming of aquatic organisms for human consumption
Arctic Circle: a line of latitude around Earth at 66°30' N
autonomous: self-governing
bureaucracy: an administrative system with a defined structure and complex rules
cede: to give control or possession of something
civil war: a conflict between citizens within the same country
coniferous: trees that produce cones and stay green all year
crusade: a military expedition, often for religious purposes
deciduous: trees that lose their leaves in autumn and grow new leaves in spring
elevation: the height of an area of land above sea level
ethnic: relating to a race or national group of people
European Union (EU): a political and economic organization, established in 1993, that has more than two dozen member countries
exported: sold goods to other countries
fish landings: the catches of marine fish landed in ports
geothermal: relating to the internal heat of Earth
gross domestic product (GDP): the total value of goods and services produced in a country or area
Gulf Stream: a current of warm water that flows from the Caribbean region across the Atlantic Ocean to northern Europe
head of state: the chief public representative of a country
hydroelectricity: electricity produced by the fast movement of water through a turbine
immigration: the act of coming to a new country to live and work
imports: buys goods from other countries
Indigenous people: people native to a certain area
lichens: plant-like organisms that grow on solid surfaces
nationalism: identification with one's own nation and support for its interests
northern lights: a display of shimmering lights that appears in the night sky in the Northern Hemisphere
occupation: a condition in which territory is under the effective control of a foreign armed force
parallel: the same distance apart along the entire length
parliamentary democracy: a type of government in which the citizens elect representatives to parliament
rapids: parts of a river where the water moves very fast, often over rocks
republic: a form of government in which a state is ruled by representatives of the citizen body
sauna: a Finnish steam bath created by pouring water on hot stones
service industries: businesses that do work for a customer but are not involved in manufacturing
species: a group of living things with similar attributes
Stone Age: a prehistoric period of human development in which stone tools were used
urban: related to cities and towns

Index

Get the best of both worlds.

AV2 bridges the gap between print and digital.

The expandable resources toolbar enables quick access to content including **videos**, **audio**, **activities**, **weblinks**, **slideshows**, **quizzes**, and **key words**.

Animated videos make static images come alive.

Resource icons on each page help readers to further **explore key concepts**.

Published by Lightbox Learning Inc.
276 5th Avenue, Suite 704 #917
New York, NY 10001
Website: www.openlightbox.com

Copyright ©2024 Lightbox Learning Inc.
All rights reserved. No part of this publication may be reproduced, stored in a retrieval system, or transmitted in any form or by any means, electronic, mechanical, photocopying, recording, or otherwise, without the prior written permission of the publisher.

Library of Congress Control Number: 2022951630

ISBN 978-1-7911-4727-3 (hardcover)
ISBN 978-1-7911-4728-0 (softcover)
ISBN 978-1-7911-4729-7 (multi-user eBook)

Printed in Guangzhou, China
1 2 3 4 5 6 7 8 9 0 27 26 25 24 23

022023
101322

Project Coordinator Heather Kissock
Designer Terry Paulhus

Photo Credits
Every reasonable effort has been made to trace ownership and to obtain permission to reprint copyright material. The publisher would be pleased to have any errors or omissions brought to its attention so that they may be corrected in subsequent printings. The publisher acknowledges Getty Images, Alamy, Minden Pictures, Shutterstock, and Wikimedia as its primary image suppliers for this title.

View new titles and product videos at www.openlightbox.com